The 3 Levels of Kingdom Provision

By

Veronica Snowden

Copyright

Unless otherwise indicated, all scripture is from the King James & New King James Versions of The Bible.

The 3 Levels of Kingdom Provision

ISBN-979-8218-21728-0

Veronica Snowden Publishing

Quincy, IL 62301-0001

For more information about Veronica Snowden Ministries or for permissions requests, email faithwaysolutions@gmail.com or visit www.veronicasnowdenministries.com

Disclaimer

The contents of the book, "Veronica Snowden Ministries," published by Veronica Snowden Publishing, and the accompanying website, www.veronicasnowden.com, are based on the author's personal experiences and examples from the Bible, specifically the King James Version. The success and outcomes you achieve in your life will depend on various factors, including your confession, belief, time spent reading the Bible, prayer in the Spirit for wisdom and guidance, and the development, application, and reliance on your faith.

It is important to note that the author's life transformation was not solely a result of hearing the Word but rather applying the teachings from the Word to their own life. Any results mentioned in this book are directly attributed to the author's trust in God and the implementation of Biblical financial principles.

However, it is crucial that readers understand that everyone's journey is unique, and individual outcomes may vary. Therefore, it is strongly advised to seek God for wisdom and personalized strategies regarding kingdom provision. The information presented in this book is intended to provide insights and guidance but should not be considered a substitute for seeking personalized counsel or professional advice.

The author, Veronica Snowden Ministries, Veronica Snowden Publishing, and the website www.veronicasnowden.com cannot be held responsible for any decisions or actions taken based on the information presented in this book. The readers are solely responsible for their choices and should exercise discernment and wisdom in applying any teachings or principles discussed.

By reading this book and utilizing the information provided, you acknowledge and accept that the author, publisher, and website are not liable for any consequences, losses, or damages that may occur as a result of your interpretation, application, or reliance on the contents of this book.

Please consult appropriate professionals or seek divine guidance in matters of finance, spirituality, and personal development, as each individual's circumstances may require personalized attention.

Remember, your journey towards kingdom provision is a unique and personal one, and this book is intended to be a tool to help you navigate that path.

Dedication

To The Body of Christ & Those Who Support Us In Teaching Kingdom Living Worldwide

My hope for you is that this book will cause a shift in your thinking, for it is within one's thoughts that their beliefs are shaped. As you speak your beliefs, you walk in the direction your beliefs lead you. The result of your life is a sum of your beliefs put into action. The power to change your life lies within your belief system. I'm so thankful to God for giving us the ability to renew our minds. May you prosper as your soul (where your mind lies) prospers by submitting to the Spirit of God (3 John 1:2). Transformation starts here.

Contents

Introduction

Have you ever found yourself struggling to make ends meet? Have you ever wondered if there's more to life than just barely getting by? As human beings, we have a natural desire for security and provision. We want to know that we will have enough to meet our needs, take care of our families, and live fulfilling lives.

But where does that provision come from? Is it up to us to work hard and make things happen for ourselves? Or does God provide an alternative way for His children? As believers, we know God has a plan for our lives and wants to provide for us. But what does that really mean?

In this book, we will explore the Three Levels of Kingdom Provision: Needs, The Blessing & Sustainability, and Divine Wealth. We will look at how God provides for His children, using examples from the Bible, and we will examine the role of money in our lives.

But more than that, we will explore how one's deep emotional attachment to money impacts Kingdom provision. We will discuss the dangers of making money our god, and how seeking God for wisdom and discernment can lead to increase in our finances.

Ultimately, we will discover that true elevation comes from God and that by acknowledging Him as the source of our provision, we can experience a level of abundance that goes beyond what we could ever imagine. So, let's dive in and explore the depths of God's provision together.

Chapter 1

Understanding The

Three Levels of Provision

What prompted me to write this book was an experience I witnessed with someone who's dear to me. I was traveling to visit this person because they were going through a situation that required financial support. The water pipes in their home had burst. They did not have water to bathe, cook, clean, or drink. There was a water shortage throughout the city. Their local power company started issuing rolling blackouts to conserve power and prevent widespread losses due to icy weather. In addition, their phone had been cut off because they could not pay the bill, and they needed groceries and drinking water for the household.

When I arrived with resources, they shared all they had been through with me. When they finished sharing, I responded by saying, "God will provide." Their response to me was, "He already did." They went on to share how they asked God to help them. They were able to use free wifi to contact a family member to pay their phone bill. Their neighbor allowed them to shower and fill a bucket of water so they could clean their home, and God sent me to supply the other resources they needed.

This believer's testimony prompted me to ask God some questions about provision. I understood about paying tithes so God could bless our money and sustain us. I even understood sowing seeds for increase, abundant living, and the ability to bless others. This has been my practice for more than twenty years. But I didn't understand how their needs were met regardless of them paying tithes or sowing seeds. I also didn't understand why God responded so quickly. Now, I know this person is a Christian, and they always give to others in need when they have extra. There were times I needed their support, and they were there for me. I asked God to help me understand. He told me that He provides for the needs of all His children. It's not based on tithe and sowing seeds; it's based on His promise to us. He said when His children cry out to Him in need, He hears them and answers them. Then God took me to the Bible to show me some examples.

Remember when Adam and Eve sinned and hid themselves because they knew they were naked? Although they clearly went against the will of God and had to leave the Garden of Eden, God still had compassion for them. He knew they were ashamed; they were naked and hid because they told Him, so God provided clothes for them.

How about the children of Israel, they were constantly complaining, doubting God, and even worshiping manmade gods. God addressed their sin but also continued to provide for them when they cried out to Him for help. He was a cloud by day so they wouldn't get too hot, a pillar of fire by night so they could see and not get too cold, and their shoes never wore out. God provided manna for them to eat daily and even gave them quail when they said they were tired of manna. Even though quail was given because of all their complaining, and God was not pleased with their grumbling, He still provided what they asked for. The key word here is "asked." The Bible says in James 4:2-3 that we have not because we ask not. Now God doesn't want us to ask amiss, but asking for provision for needs is not asking amiss. We must make our requests known to God. The Bible tells us to in Philippians 4:6-8. Many Christians believe they shouldn't ask God for things because God already knows everything and what they need, but that's not true. There are several verses throughout the Bible where God tells us to ask Him for what we need.

I remember a couple of times when I had no food to eat. My fridge was bare. I was just starting to rebuild my life after a separation. I said, "God I'm hungry. I need something to eat." Later, when I got to work that night, I was blessed with twenty dollars for lunch. They had no idea that I had a conversation with God about it. But when they gave me the money, they specifically said it was for me to get something to eat. God heard my request. He saw I was in need and responded immediately. I can attest to countless times God has acted in my time of need. I would only talk to God about my needs or concerns; then He would influence a man or a situation to show me He heard me and was answering my call.

At this point, I felt the need to ask God to forgive me for having a religious mindset and for showing me that He provides for all His children's needs when they call on Him. He told me I wasn't wrong about why we pay tithes and sow seeds, that those are different categories of provision.

We've all heard or read the scripture in the Bible that states, "My God shall supply all your needs according to His riches and glory in Christ Jesus (Philippians 4:19). Then another scripture that says bring all your tithes into the storehouse that there might be food in My house, and try Me now in this, says the Lord of hosts, "If I will not open the windows of heaven and pour out for you such a blessing that there will not be room enough to receive it," (Malachi 3:10). Deuteronomy 8:18 says Remember the Lord thy God, for it is He who gives you the power to get wealth, that He may establish His covenant that he swore to your fathers, as it is this day. Looking at each verse, we will notice three different types of provision. One verse talks about needs, the following verse talks about the connection between the blessing, paying tithes, and trying God in the area of finances to sustain us, and the last verse talks about God giving us the power to get wealth to establish His covenant. You see each of the three types of provision throughout the Bible, not just in one or two places. That's when I got the revelation that kingdom provision is just like faith; there are different levels.

As I reflected for a bit, I realized that I had experienced all three levels of provision: needs, the blessing with sustainability & Divine wealth (which means I have more than enough to sustain my lifestyle (which includes leisure activities such as travel or buying a third vehicle, investing, and saving money, etc.) while still being a blessing to others, paying my tithes, offerings, sowing seeds and without having to work overtime, two jobs or needing any assistance: government, family, friends, credit cards, etc.).

Now I'm sharing the three levels with you. We will take a deeper look at each level to allow you to gain a clear understanding of each type of provision, so you can determine which one you are on and how you transition to the next level if you desire. I will also share my personal story and the practical kingdom strategy that I implemented to assist you with transitioning from one level to the next.

Chapter 2

God Created You to Provide for You

Have you ever felt lost, helpless, or alone? Have you ever been in a situation where you had no idea how you were going to make it through? If so, then you know how it feels to need provision. But what if I told you that God created you intending to provide for you?

From the beginning of time, God has been providing for His children. In the Bible (the Old Testament & New Testament), we see numerous examples of how God provided for His people, whether it was food, water, protection, guidance, or money. The Israelites in the wilderness are a prime example of this. God provided them with manna, quail, and water from a rock to sustain them during their journey. There is one part of this story that is overlooked when it's shared in church. In Exodus 12:32-36 you will find that Pharaoh told the children of Israel to take their flocks and herds; and granted their request to take articles of gold, silver, and clothing. The Word actually says they plundered the Egyptians. Plunder means to strip the Egyptians of their wealth. The children of Israel did not go into the wilderness broke.

But kingdom provision isn't just limited to physical needs. God also provides for us emotionally and spiritually. He offers comfort and peace during times of trouble and wisdom and guidance during decision-making. All we have to do is turn to Him and trust His plan.

I remember a time in my life when I was going through a wilderness. I felt lost and alone, with no idea how to move forward. But when I turned to God, He provided for me in ways I never imagined. He gave me peace in the midst of my struggle and provided me with the strength and guidance I needed to overcome my challenges.

Why does God provide for us? Because He loves us and wants the best for us. God created us with a purpose and a plan, and part of that plan includes providing for our needs and desires. When we turn to God for provision, we are acknowledging that He is the source of all provision. We are placing our trust in Him, knowing that God has the solution to our problems, not man and not always money.

So, if you need provision today, whether physical, emotional, or spiritual, turn to God. He created you intending to provide for you, and He will never leave you or forsake you. Trust in Him and His plan for your life, and watch as He provides for you in ways you never thought possible.

Chapter 3

Money Is Just a Tool: God Is the Source

Money is just a tool. It is essential that believers understand its purpose. In the last chapter, we talked about God being the solution to our problems, not man, and not always money. I know this may sound contradictory, so I wanted to use this chapter to explain how God wants us to view money. God created money as a tool to be used by man. He didn't intend for us to glorify it, compromise who we are to have it, or let it be the motivation behind what we do to obtain it. By doing this, we make money, our god, and you will always be chasing it. But if you see God as your source and not money, then you stop having to chase it but influence it to come to you by staying at the feet of God and seeking Him for wisdom, discernment, and provision for your situation.

If we are honest with ourselves, it's not the money we seek but the lifestyle it affords us. If someone came to you and said you could have whatever lifestyle you want and not have to worry about using any money with no strings attached, you would accept it. God wants you to see Him as your source, not your job, people, or a business but Him. God doesn't mind you having a job. Some people feel called to a specific job or business.

Now let's address the verse that's led many Christians to believe that having a lot of money is evil. The Bible does say the love of money is the root of all evil (1 Timothy 6:10) because it is. Root means the source, the starting point of evil (sin or corruption).

We shouldn't be loving money; it's not even alive. We should love the Creator of money. Love God. Make God your source, and the money will come automatically. In a later chapter, we will discuss what happens when you make money your God.

In Matthew 6:25-33, Jesus says, "Therefore I tell you, do not worry about your life, what you will eat or drink; or about your body, what you will wear. Is not life more than food and the body more than clothes? Look at the birds of the air; they do not sow or reap or store away in barns, and yet your heavenly Father feeds them. Are you not much more valuable than they?" God's Word says to seek Him first, the kingdom of God and all His righteousness, and all these things shall be added unto you. Money is a thing, right? So that means if I seek first the Kingdom of God and not the world's way of doing things, money will be added to me.

I remember trying to obtain a job by getting a "hook-up," also known as a referral, from a friend. That's typically how it's done in the world, right? Well, my friend returned to me and told me they couldn't get me the job. I was upset about it. I really wanted that job. I decided to go to God about it. Sometimes I tend to go to God second instead of first concerning my life. God has been teaching me to get aligned with the Word first so I can save myself the stress and worry. I asked Him why I didn't get the job. He told me that elevation should come from Him so that He could get the glory. I cried and repented. I didn't realize I was putting my hope in man to get me a job and not God. How would God get the glory? What would my testimony be, "I got this job because my friend hooked me up," I don't see God in that statement. God wants to be involved in the beginning, throughout the process, and at the end when we are victorious so he can get the glory.

A job is a type of provision, so God wants to be involved. I ended up getting a lower-paying position but told God in secret that I still desired the position that I wasn't able to get. Six months passed, and I was offered that exact position that my friend couldn't get me. I never even applied for it. I didn't even interview for it. The assistant campus director told my manager to inform my supervisors that I would be offered the position. My supervisors didn't particularly care for me, so they would not have offered me the position, so God bypassed them. All glory goes to God.

God knows that money can be a major concern; that's why he tells you not to worry and to seek Him first, His way of doing things. He sees what we can't see and knows what and who needs to be moved around to get us what we have been asking for. And yes, there were times I didn't get what I was asking for, but I usually find out later that it may have been harmful to me, or God had something better in store for me. If we, being humans, care about giving our children good gifts, don't you think God cares, even more, to give His children good things if we ask? (Matthew. 7:11)

Chapter 4

The First Level of Provision: Needs

The first level of provision is needs. We all know about needs; it's your bare necessities. This includes things like food, shelter, and clothing. These are the things that we need to survive. But I will explain how believers' needs are met through the kingdom of God. At this level, believers are still on milk spiritually (the beginning level of faith to believe for kingdom provision). They are either developing their faith for finances, have not been taught or trained in the area of finances, or simply refuse to believe (still doubt) that God can and wants to provide for them financially beyond their needs. Provision of needs is when a believer may not be paying tithes regularly but gives at times and in other ways. Still, it's only enough to make it. The believer is not getting ahead. Their money fluctuates because it is still in the cursed world. It will always be limited if it remains in the world system.

Many believers struggle at this level because they are not fully committed to trusting God with and for their finances. They have yet to learn to develop their faith in the area of finances. They have yet to understand kingdom principles for giving and receiving, sowing and reaping, and seed time and harvest. As a result, their financial situation remains stagnant, and they are just getting by from paycheck to paycheck and may require and request assistance from others to survive.

But the good news is that God is a provider. Even though He knows what we need before we ask, God wants us to ask Him. The Bible says we have not because we don't ask. We must make our requests known to God. Many Christians believe they shouldn't do this because God knows everything, but that belief does not align with what the Word of God tells us to do. The Bible tells us in several verses to ask God. I always look for two to three witnesses (two to three scriptures to support what I'm believing God for). James 4:2-3, Matt 7:7-12 and Philippians 4:6-7 are three scriptures you can reference. We must open our mouths and say what we want. I think about my children in relation to this. Every time we go to the store, they want something, they always do. Sometimes my answer may be no, but many times my answer is yes if they ask me. I may know my child wants a particular doll or treat because I know my child, but they may not get it if they don't ask me. I need them to communicate with me like God wants us to communicate with Him. Psalms 84:11 Says the

Lord will give grace and glory, and no good thing will He withhold from them that walk uprightly.

Remember I said you are a spiritual baby on milk at the needs level? When your baby cries, what do you do? You go get their bottle, check their diaper, see if they are sleepy, and so on. The point is you respond to their cry. God does the same thing. He responds to our cry (when we call out to God) for help, and He provides for our needs.

Although this is where believers start, He doesn't want us to stay at this level. God doesn't want us to live in lack, poverty or only to make ends meet. He wants us to operate in abundance and overflow. God wants us to receive the riches Jesus went to the cross for. He wants us to advance the kingdom of God and be a blessing to others. So, let's move on to the second level of provision: the blessing & sustainability.

Chapter 5

Should We Believe God for Money?

I added this chapter before the second level of provision because many Christians have a conflict with asking God for money above their needs. Someone recently told me they don't want to ask God for too much and use up all their blessings. I said to them that you couldn't use up something God intended for us to have. Kingdom provision is part of the covenant God made with Abraham that extends to the Body of Christ today. God is happy when you come to Him and see Him as your source. Now let's discuss if we should believe God for money.

I'm just going to be honest. Many believers have been taught that we shouldn't seek God for money, that money is evil, and that God and money should be kept separate. But how do you separate a creation from its Creator? On earth, this happens all the time. People will steal another's idea, product, or invention without giving them any credit. Well, believe it or not, believers do this when they say money is evil or mock prosperity teaching and say Christians shouldn't seek God for money. As you continue to read you will begin to understand what I mean by God not getting the credit.

Here's a thought-provoking question: Who or what should believers be seeking money from? Should our job be our source? But what if you get fired, demoted, have a reduction in pay, or even worse, lose your ability to work? Oh, I know; maybe getting a government check is the answer. This country has really been pushing socialism lately. Do you really want the government to be your source of income? We all know a few somebodies who only live off a government check, and they are barely surviving, have to borrow and ask for help to cover all their monthly bills or get a part-time job (many underhandedly), or simply go without. Let's talk about running a business. Now, I actually believe in entrepreneurship. I had a few businesses in my lifetime. But what about when businesses shut down, like during Covid or the market and mortgage crash of the early 2000s? Many businesses were wiped out resulting in many losing their life savings. There was so much devastation that many committed suicide.

I know I'm asking a lot of questions. But this chapter was written to help you rethink how you see God and money. Let's just get this straight regardless if you ever choose to believe God for money. God created money. Gold and silver are money (Today, we mainly use the paper form of money or plastic). Satan did not create money. He does not have that ability. He can deceive and manipulate people to believe that He controls money; therefore, people believe him and think they must go through him, the world's way to get it. Everything God created is good, so money is good. It's people with bad intentions, dealings, and greed that are evil and corrupt. So, you know who their god is. God created money for His children to take care of themselves, the earth, the poor and needy, the widow and children, to advance the Kingdom of God, and to draw back home His lost children.

I have tried doing it the world's way countless times and always came up short. I had to compromise my time and my body (working long hours, not getting enough sleep, wear and tear on my joints, I took a flu shot against my beliefs because it became "law" in my state for healthcare workers), took less pay than I thought I deserved, and many other things that caused me to stress about money.

When I lost my ability to work in 2012, I was so scared about my family's financial future. I didn't think it was responsible to have children and not work to take care of them. I always thought those types of people were lazy. I was willing to work hard for my children, but my physical condition and my doctor wouldn't allow me to. My only option left was God. I couldn't get a loan. I had no way of paying it back. My husband, at the time, was so inconsistent with paying the bills so I couldn't depend on him. I was used to providing my own way, taking care of myself, so I thought. I cried out to God because I didn't know what else to do. God heard my cry. He reminded me how he took care of me before my fall from grace with sin. I said, "But God, this is different; It's not just me. I have children who are depending on me now." I'm used to having some type of a job, even if it's low paying." "This time I had no job, no savings, but two new responsibilities (twin boys), and the doctors still hadn't released me to work because my physical condition hadn't changed since having my twins a year prior. God asked me straight up, "Am I your source?" I replied yes. Then He said put your eyes back on Me to provide and watch Me take care of you and your babies without a job. I was thinking, "What? Really? Now that's another level for me, but ok, God, I will trust you." That day changed my life and how I see God regarding money. I have been believing God for money ever since, and He has provided without fail.

Chapter 6

The Second Level: The Blessing & Sustainability

The second level of provision is the blessing & sustainability. On this level, believers start to experience the true power of the kingdom in the area of finances. They began transitioning from milk to meat as they apply the Word to their lives by faith. They are not simply getting their needs met. They are experiencing abundance and overflow. Believers are typically paying tithes and offering regularly. They understand the importance of applying their faith, advancing the kingdom of God, and taking the financial burden of caring for themselves and placing it on God by trusting Him with their finances.

One of the most significant benefits of this level is the supernatural transfer that takes place. Your money leaves the cursed world to enter the kingdom of God and comes back to you blessed. This is what I call experiencing the miracle of distribution and increase. There is no requirement to work overtime, work two jobs, or have a side hustle to survive at this level. I call it laundering or cleaning your money spiritually, lol (laugh out loud). You do not see how your money is increased; that's why it's called a miracle. As you give God the first 10%, the 90% that remains is blessed as well. It will increase to function at 100%, 110%, and even 120% if needed. Although I cannot see how it's done, I have experienced the benefit countless times.

I cannot tell you how many times I did not have enough money in my physical bank account or cash, yet the bills somehow were always paid without me working more hours or requesting assistance from anyone but God. Your lifestyle is sustained at that level even if you don't have a job or a business. As I'm writing this book, I have not been working for the last six months (I resigned from nursing to homeschool my child that was struggling in the public school system), yet my lifestyle has been sustained without any type of assistance. To be transparent, I receive $550 a month as a form of support for my children. Believe me, I'm grateful. Every bit of income is a blessing, but I want to show that this amount is not sufficient to cover all my bills. I still have a mortgage, two vehicles with a lease payment, homeschool tuition for my child, and other monthly maintenance bills. Plus, I also like to travel. So how am I sustained with three children? The answer is the blessing (studying the Word, being obedient with paying my tithes and offerings and other Kingdom financial principles for increase). I pay my tithe (yes, I tithe off the $550 even though I didn't earn it). All money that comes into my hands gets spiritually laundered from the curse to the blessing. I pay offerings, I sow financial seeds for increase, and I give to those who are less fortunate. Then I trust God to perform His Word just as He promised, and He does, time, after time.

The level of the blessing & sustainability is more than just about meeting your needs. It is about experiencing the true power of the blessing of the Kingdom when it comes to finances. It is about trusting God with your money and allowing Him to bless it and multiply it beyond what you could ever imagine. So, if you are still on the first level, take heart and continue to develop your faith and apply kingdom financial principles as you seek the Holy Spirit for guidance. You will soon find yourself experiencing the supernatural provision and sustainability of the Kingdom. By now, you may be thinking, "Can it get any better?" Yes, it can. It is great to be sustained, especially in the world we live in today. But God wants us to be more than sustained; He wants us to be increased so that we will have more than enough for ourselves, our family, and be positioned financially to act when He needs us to. God wants us to be able to be a blessing to others as well as advance the Kingdom of God without our way of life being affected at all. The third level is when the believer becomes blessed to be a blessing. Now it is time to learn about divine wealth. Let's head over to the next chapter.

Chapter 7

The Third Level: Divine Wealth

The third level of provision is divine wealth, which is where believers have developed a level of faith to go beyond just paying tithes and offerings. They understand how giving and sowing seeds into good ground increases them financially. At this level, sowing a seed is not just about giving money; it is about investing in the Kingdom of God to advance the Body of Christ as well as increase your financial position. It is not just about getting your needs met or sustaining your lifestyle, but it's about wanting to see others prosper as well. Financial wealth is the by-product.

A seed can be sown in the form of physical money (which is the typical way), but it can also be in the form of a word seed, vision seed, or something else that God may lead you to do. The key is to be obedient to God's leading and sow into good ground, which will result in a supernatural financial return on your giving.

Sowing seeds is not an alternative to paying tithes and offerings; it is an addition to it. Tithes and offerings are the foundation of financial provision, and sowing seeds is an advanced level of giving that builds on that foundation. When you give to advance the Kingdom of God, both you and the Kingdom benefit.

An example of sowing a seed for divine wealth provision is when I sowed into my pastor and first lady's personal ministry. This is separate and different from sowing a seed to their church. This is sowing into the lives of a man and woman of God because you believe God has used them to be a blessing to your life. This was during a time in my life when I was believing God for financial increase, but I only had enough to put a financial seed in the ground. I was believing for the finances to travel to the UK for a semester to study international music business. This was not considered needs provision or the blessing and sustainability. All my needs were met, my bills were paid, and my lifestyle was sustained. This was a desire that I wanted God to finance. Shortly after sowing my seed, within thirty days, God gave me favor with several people who financially supported my desire.

Sowing seeds not only benefit you financially, but it also blesses others. About a year ago, a similar situation happened to me where someone came to sow (blessed me with a financial seed) in my life because they were believing for a home of their own. They saw me as good ground because I demonstrated that I live by faith. Within one year, they were able to purchase a new home for themselves.

In the kingdom of God, to elevate financially, we must plant a seed into good ground, ground that has already produced the type of harvest we are believing for. Sowing seeds is not only a way for believers to increase themselves financially, but we are also able to be a blessing to others while advancing the Kingdom of God. In the next chapter, I will share my personal story in more detail of how God provided for my trip to the UK through sowing seeds.

Chapter 8

My UK Story: Divine Provision & Increase

My story of divine provision and increase transformed my thinking about how I see God concerning my finances and if I should seek Him for money. It was a life-changing experience that taught me the true power of sowing seeds and trusting God for my financial breakthrough.

When I was believing to go overseas to the UK, I did not have enough money to pay for travel from Memphis, TN to Chicago (where I needed to go to catch an international flight), the round-trip plane ticket to the UK, the money for housing, food, and just general financial support. I was going as a foreign exchange student to study international music business for a semester. I was only going to be overseas for four and a half months, so I was not allowed to work (you must be overseas for at least six months to qualify for a Visa to work). Although I had heard the message of sowing seeds for increase many times, this particular time in church, my pastor was preaching about it, and it stuck with me. All I had in my bank account at that time was between $386 and $400. I cannot remember precisely, so I rounded it to $400, Lol. I did not sow the seed at first. I left church service that day and let it marinate in me. I talked to my boyfriend at the time about it. He told me I should not give all I had left to the church because I needed it and already didn't have enough. Thinking naturally, I can see why he would say that. My boyfriend was not speaking to me as a man of faith. He was talking to me as a man that operated through His natural mind and senses for understanding, which will not profit us if we want to grow financially through the Spirit. The sermon's title was "If I don't have enough for what I need, it must be a seed." I looked at my bank account, then looked at where I was trying to go but did not have the money to take me there in my physical account. That was a clear sign that this message was for me.

Nothing else was working in the natural, and I was running out of time. My trip was thirty days or less away, and I was desperate. In Philippians 4:6, God tells us to be anxious for nothing but with everything in prayer and supplication, let our requests be made known to Him. God also tells us to try Him in the areas of tithes and offerings in Malachi 3:10. I figured, why not try Him with my finances to study overseas. I am so thankful I had already experienced God increasing me through the vehicle of faith. This was just my first time putting a physical, financial seed in the ground to put a demand on my kingdom inheritance. This was another level of faith for me. I decided to put my seed in the ground. I made sure I named my seed (I wrote on the back of the envelope what I was believing for). The first lady called me to thank me for sowing into her ministry, then got into the prayer of agreement with me. The Bible says when two or three come together and agree on anything on earth, He is in the midst, and they shall have whatever they ask for—within thirty days of us praying, my $400 seed turned into a $6,000 plus return. It is the opposite of the world system, where you get a small return of less than 1% or 7 to 10% if you put a lot of money in upfront.

God covered all my expenses for the entire semester abroad. I even came back to the States with the remainder of $1,000 in my bank account. I was in awe of God's goodness and faithfulness. All glory went to Him because, otherwise, my trip would not have happened.

Looking back, I realize that sowing that seed was not just about receiving kingdom financial provision. It was also about trusting God and growing my faith. It was a reminder that God is my provider and that He is always faithful to His promises.

Since then, I have continued to build and apply my faith, sow seeds into good ground and trust God for my financial increase. I have seen supernatural provision in my life, and I am grateful that my God not only cares for my needs but my desires as well.

If you are facing a financial obstacle and unsure what to do, I encourage you to seek God for wisdom and ask God to let your heart be sensitive to hear His guidance. Ask Him to show you when and where you should sow your seed to ensure it is good ground. If you do not have a seed, ask God to supply it. The Bible says God supplies seed to the sower (2 Corinthians 9:10).

When you sow a seed, you are not just investing money; you are applying your faith, the Word of God, to your life. You are trusting God with your finances for divine provision and financial increase. When you see God perform His Word from your sacrificial seed, you cannot help but give God the glory and share your story to help encourage someone else. It is a win for the Kingdom, and it's a win for you. Everybody wins when you elevate God's way. That is how we roll (how things are done) in the Kingdom of God.

Chapter 9

When Money Becomes Your God

In chapter three, we talked about money being just a tool and God being the source. Now we will dive deeper and discuss the dangers of loving money and making it your god. Money is a resource, not a source, so you can't depend on it to take care of you. It cannot talk to you or give you the answer to your financial struggles. It cannot tell you where you can find it or give you an unlimited supply of itself. Yet you have many people, the world, as well as believers worshiping money.

Worshipping isn't new to God. The Children of Israel were worshiping money in the wilderness. They made a golden calf with the gold that God allowed them to strip from the Egyptians, so they could worship something they could see with their physical eyes. This was a belief system the children of Israel developed in Egypt (the world's way of doing things). Because they had been in slavery for so long, they had forgotten the way of their Fathers: Abraham, Isaac & Jacob, who left the land of pagan gods to follow a God they could not see but believed and acted by faith. Just imagine how God felt. He made sure the Children of Israel didn't leave Egypt broke by providing them with gold, silver, clothing, and livestock. Yet, they still desired to worship a manmade god, something they created, instead of Worshiping the one who created and delivered them?

When you make money your god, you open yourself up for Satan to influence your decisions concerning money. It becomes your motive behind everything you do. You will do anything to get it and anything to keep it. This is the reason people rob, cheat, lie, break the law, and kill to get it. People have even taken their own lives because they lost everything financially. There is only one who comes to steal, kill, and destroy, and that is Satan. He is influencing these actions. Many believers will stay at a horrible job, in a toxic relationship, and compromise their beliefs just for money. I've seen people start businesses just for the money. They don't even like or use the product or service they are selling. They are controlled by money and have become a slave to it. That's the worse position to be in.

When Satan knows you will do anything to have money, he knows he can get you to sell your soul for it. I know that sounds harsh, but people do it every day. What really grieves my heart is when a believer leaves the faith for money that they feel they can only get from the world. But the truth is the money that Satan dangles in believers' faces already belongs to them. They just don't know it because many preachers are not teaching it in the church. They don't realize they can have wealth with God without compromising their faith.

It's unbelievable how many people are working hard to produce wealth on their own, regardless if it's legal, illegal, or unethical, when God already knows where the money is and how to get it to you because He created it. Yet if you see a believer with money, some Christians will think or even say, "They must be doing something underhanded." "They couldn't possibly be getting that type of money with only God being their source." What a slap in God's face. He created it but can't get it to you?

God shouldn't be compartmentalized to only being the God of your spiritual life. He wants to be the God of your everyday life as well. Whatever concerns you concerns, God, and He wants you to come to Him about it so He can help you by giving you a solution. And yes, that includes money. God doesn't want you to make money your god because when you do, you give Satan the legal right to be your god, and, in the end, he will use it to destroy you. He has to take it back because it doesn't belong to him legally. It belongs to the Body of Christ. It's part of our Kingdom inheritance, but we must go to God to get it and keep it without compromising our faith.

In Matthew 6:24, Jesus says, "No one can serve two masters. Either you will hate the one and love the other, or you will be devoted to the one and despise the other. You cannot serve both God and money."

I'm just going to keep this simple and to the point. Money was created to serve us, and we were created to serve God. Because God gave us the authority, we should be telling money what to do. It should not dictate what we do. We should value God above money.

What we do with our money determines our understanding of the Kingdom of God and how much we value and trust God in the area that's most dear to us, our finances. Do we pay tithes and offering to advance the Kingdom of God? Do we sow into others' lives financially? Do we give to the widow and their children, the poor and sick? Are we just trying to get money for ourselves, or are we looking for ways to impact others' lives financially?

I remember turning down a job because it conflicted with me attending Sunday morning service. God had that same company call me back and offer me a position that allowed me to be off on Sunday. I remember being the only person at another job to be allowed to come in late so that I wouldn't miss Sunday morning service. I also left a job that allowed me to bring in six figures that year because I refused to compromise my beliefs to take a Covid shot. Two months later, that job called me back to offer me a position they created that would allow me to sign a waiver of exemption. Why did I share all this? I want you to know I'm not telling you to do something I heard or read somewhere. I want you to know that I have personally experienced the same financial challenges. I am showing you when you put God first and see Him as your source and not money; you do not have to go without it. You still get to have it. You just do not have to compromise your beliefs to get it and God gets the glory because you honored Him as your source, not money.

Chapter 10

Why Satan Doesn't Want Believers to Prosper

Satan has always been against the prosperity of God's children. He doesn't want us to prosper financially because it means we will no longer need to depend on the world's system but will become completely reliant on God. This will cause Satan's kingdom to collapse. The world only needs Satan because they are unaware that they can have the same thing in the kingdom of God without sacrificing lives and dignity to get it. They are not aware because most of the Body of Christ is not aware to tell them. The Body of Christ is unaware because very few ministers teach it. This is why Satan works continuously to negatively influence believers' minds and hinder them through physical circumstances when we try to pay tithes, offerings, or sow seeds. He wants Christians to believe that these principles don't work and that we will never be able to prosper financially by doing things God's way.

If Satan can keep believers from learning about the financial Kingdom principles, then he can continue to have a hold on the financial industry. The world's financial system is designed to keep people in debt, working long hours, and always striving to make ends meet. But God's Kingdom principles are designed to free us from that bondage and allow us to prosper in every area of our lives. Satan is ok if a few of us Believers know as long as the masses don't.

Satan wants believers to struggle financially or utilize self-determination without God, so when you rise to a certain level, he has the legal right to take over whatever wealth you have built. He will use people and circumstances in an attempt to hinder your faith. But we must remember that God is not only with us but is also in us. With God, we will win in every situation and over the enemy. Remember to hold fast to our faith and confession and listen to the Spirit for guidance. We need to stay focused on the promises of God and not the problems before our eyes. They are all just distractions. God's word is truth, and He is faithful to perform it. We just need to believe in Him and ask God to show us His promises in the Word and give us peace about it.

As we learn about kingdom financial principles in the Word, we must apply them to our lives by faith. Then we need to follow the guidance of the Holy Spirit in our hearts. Initially, it may seem like it's not working, but don't stop, because it is. Continue to stand on your faith and watch God bring you to a place of financial prosperity that Satan can never touch.

Let's Wrap It Up

As we conclude our exploration of the three levels of provision, we are left with a sense of awe and wonder at the grace and love of our Heavenly Father. We have seen how God is not only interested in meeting our basic needs but desires to increase us as we apply the Word to our lives by faith. God is the ultimate provider, and when we acknowledge Him as the source of our provision, we open ourselves up to financial abundance and The Blessing in our lives.

Understanding the three levels of kingdom provision - needs, the blessing & sustainability, and divine wealth - is crucial to understanding how God provides for His children. By acknowledging God as the source of all provision and understanding money is just a tool, we can avoid the dangers of making money our god and instead seek God for wisdom and discernment in increasing our finances. Ultimately, we must utilize kingdom financial principles for increase that align with the Word of God and understand that elevation should come from God so that He will get the glory in the end. No man, business, or level of education should get the credit that's due to God.

Through studying examples from the Word, we can see how God has provided for His children throughout history, and we (the Body of Christ) can still trust in His provision for us today. I'm a living witness, and so are many other believers. As we seek to live by the Word of God and follow His kingdom financial principles for increase, we can experience the fullness of provision in our lives, from meeting our basic needs to experiencing the abundance of divine wealth.

Prayer For Salvation Through Jesus Christ

God, you said in John 3:16 that You so loved the world that You gave Your only begotten Son that whosoever believes in Him shall not perish but shall have everlasting life. You said in Romans 10: 9 & 10 that If we confess with our mouth that Jesus died on the cross for our sins and believe that You raised Him from the dead, we shall be saved. I am calling on you, Lord Jesus Christ, to save me according to Acts 2:21. I repent of my sins, and I am ready to be converted so that Your blood may blot out my sins. Jesus, I believe you are the one and true living God, the only way to Salvation. I denounce all other gods. I ask you to come into my heart, forgive me of my sins, and save me from all unrighteousness. I believe that God, the Father raised you from the dead. I receive the gift of Salvation now, In Jesus Mighty Name, Amen.

Prayer To Be Filled with The Evidence of The Holy Spirit: Speak in Tongues

God, thank You for sending the Helper (the Holy Spirit) to live in my heart, to guide me into all truth (John 16:13), provide wisdom and discernment, and to make intercession for me to You as I act on my faith. God, I thank You for the gift of the Holy Spirit. You said in Acts 2:1-3 that You will pour out Your Spirit on all flesh in the last days. You sent the Holy Spirit to live in me once I accepted the Lord Jesus as my Lord and Savior. Now I'm asking for evidence of being filled with the Holy Spirit by giving me utterance to speak in other tongues, my heavenly language, to commune with you as the Holy Spirit makes intercession for me. I now receive the gift of baptism with the evidence of the Holy Spirit (speaking in other tongues); in Jesus mighty name, I pray, Amen.

Begin to thank and praise God for giving you utterance. Speak the language that God gives you from your belly. Don't be afraid to speak what God gives you to say. It may sound funny to your natural mind. You will not be able to understand what you are saying. It will sound like a foreign tongue. Just keep speaking what God gives you to say. Continue to speak in your heavenly language daily (regularly) to edify yourself, commune with God, and be able to hear God speak to you.

Welcome to the family. Now you can head over to your local church and request to be water baptized or have a mature believer in their faith (someone you trust) to assist you with an in- home water baptism.

About Author

Veronica Snowden is a Kingdom

Living Minister, a loving mom of three beautiful children, with a career background as a Psychiatric Mental Health Nurse, songwriter & singer.

She has been implementing Kingdom Living Strategies in her life for the past twenty-plus years.

Her teachings focus on helping believers understand the mysteries of the kingdom of God so they can: discover their true kingdom identity, develop, apply, and stand on their faith to possess the promises of God, invest in the advancement of the Kingdom of

God, bring in the harvest, and disciple other Christians to do the same.

She currently creates digital content showing believers how to tap into their God-given greatness. Whether writing a book, entering full-time ministry, starting a business, or engaging in outreach, Veronica's mission is to empower individuals to step into their divine destiny.

Resources

To Learn More About Veronica Snowden Ministries please visit us at the following sites:

www.veronicasnowdenministries.com

Learn how to:

Grow Your Faith- Listen to Our Podcast or Read our Blog.

Upgrade Your Lifestyle- Join Our Elite Mom's Club (The Successful Single Parent Program for Single Moms)

Start Your Kingdom Business

Write Your First Book

To connect with other kingdom minded believers, go to:

group.veronicasnowdenministries.com

Join Our Free FB Group- Learn Kingdom Living Strategies

Receive FREE Subscription to Our Kingdom Living Newsletter (get access to discounts, FREE promos, giveaways, first access to all new releases)

Please Feel Free to Contact Us At VeronicaS@veronicasnowdenministries.com.

You can also find us on FB: @ Veronica Lavon

Before You Go, I Wanted to Ask You One Last Thing. If You Found This Book to Be Helpful to You in Any Way, Will You Please Head Over to Amazon & Leave Me A Review? Just Type "Veronica Snowden" Into The Amazon Search Bar To Locate "The 3 Levels of Kingdom Provision"

I Just Want to Thank You in Advance for Taking The Time Out To Do This For Me.

As Always, Be Blessed

Made in United States
Cleveland, OH
04 November 2026

47645293R00045